W9-CEH-169

LEADERSHIP THROUGH THE AGES
A COLLECTION OF FAVORITE QUOTATIONS

Copyright © 2003 Miramax Books

Introduction copyright © 2003 Rudolph W. Giuliani

ISBN 1-4013-5929-9

FIRST EDITION

10 9 8 7 6 5 4 3 2 1

E Pluribus Unum
(Out of many, one.)

—OFFICIAL MOTTO FOR THE GREAT SEAL OF
THE UNITED STATES OF AMERICA

CONTENTS

INTRODUCTION

Are leaders born or made? It's a question I am frequently asked when I speak about leadership in many parts of the world. In my opinion, the answer is that leadership is mostly a skill that people learn. They learn from their parents, from their friends and colleagues, from their teachers, and from their clergy. But leaders also learn from leaders they've never met—by reading about them. When I set out to write *Leadership*, I didn't rely on texts about management theory or academic treatises on leadership strategies. Instead, I delved into books about leaders I've long admired. In fact, I've always taken wisdom and inspiration from biographies of figures such as Winston Churchill, Thomas Jefferson, and Ronald Reagan. I have strived to adapt their circumstances to different settings and incorporate their best ideas into my own leadership style. Having read these books and many other biographies and histories sharpened my understanding of how these great leaders thought and acted. And it did something else, as well. It elevated my spirit.

This book of quotations about leadership is intended to do the same for you.

Enjoy.

—RUDOLPH W. GIULIANI

LEADERSHIP THROUGH THE AGES
A COLLECTION OF FAVORITE QUOTATIONS

CHARACTER

Faced with crisis, the man of character falls back upon himself.

—CHARLES DE GAULLE

There is a spirit and a need and a man at the beginning of every great human advance. Each of these must be right for that particular moment in history, or nothing happens.

—CORETTA SCOTT KING

Leadership is a potent combination of strategy and character. But if you must be without one, be without the strategy.

—GEN. H. NORMAN SCHWARZKOPF

Forethought and prudence are the proper qualities of a leader.

—CORNELIUS TACITUS

It is not the oath that makes us believe the man, but the man the oath.

—AESCHYLUS

There are no secrets to success: don't waste time looking for them. Success is the result of perfection, hard work, learning from failure, loyalty to those for whom you work, and persistence.

—COLIN POWELL

I desire so to conduct the affairs of this administration that if at the end, when I come to lay down the reins of power, I have lost every friend on earth, I shall at least have one friend left, and that friend shall be down inside me.

—ABRAHAM LINCOLN

Whoever is careless with the truth in small matters cannot be trusted with the important matters.

—ALBERT EINSTEIN

Sincerity and competence is a strong combination. In politics, it's everything.

—PEGGY NOONAN

It's amazing how many cares disappear when you decide not to be something, but to be someone.

—COCO CHANEL

A great city is that which has the greatest
men and women,
If it be a few ragged huts, it is still the
greatest city in the whole world.

—WALT WHITMAN

I care not what others think of what I do, but I care very much about what I think of what I do: That is character!

—THEODORE ROOSEVELT

When statesmen forsake their own private conscience for the sake of their public duties...they lead their country by a short route to chaos.

—ROBERT BOLT

Rabbi Zusya said, a short while before his death: "In the world to come I shall not be asked: 'Why were you not Moses?' I shall be asked: 'Why were you not Zusya?'"

—MARTIN BUBER

The ultimate measure of a man is not where he stands in moments of comfort and convenience, but where he stands at times of challenge and controversy.

—REV. MARTIN LUTHER KING, JR.

Genius is an infinite capacity for taking life by the scruff of the neck.

—KATHARINE HEPBURN

Nothing is more simple than greatness; indeed, to be simple is to be great.

—RALPH WALDO EMERSON

One must be something, in order to do something.

—GOETHE

No man was ever great by imitation.

—SAMUEL JOHNSON

What is the use of being elected or re-elected unless you stand for something?

—GROVER CLEVELAND

If you don't stand for something, you will stand for anything.

—GINGER ROGERS

It is a grand mistake to think of being great without goodness; and I pronounce it as certain that there was never yet a truly great man that was not at the same time truly virtuous.

—BENJAMIN FRANKLIN

Try not to become a man of success, but rather a man of value.

—ALBERT EINSTEIN

COURAGE

A man is a lion for his own cause.
—SCOTTISH PROVERB

If we take the generally accepted definition of bravery as a quality which knows no fear, I have never seen a brave man. All men are frightened. The more intelligent they are, the more they are frightened.
—GEN. GEORGE S. PATTON

Courage is resistance to fear, mastery of fear—not absence of fear. Except a creature be part coward it is not a compliment to say it is brave; it is merely a loose application of the word. Consider the flea!—incomparably the bravest of all the creatures of God, if ignorance of fear were courage.
—MARK TWAIN

Courage leads to the stars, fear toward death.
—SENECA

The weapon of the brave is in his heart.

—PROVERB

I have nothing to offer but blood, toil, tears, and sweat.

—WINSTON CHURCHILL

High sentiments always win in the end. The leaders who offer blood, toil, tears and sweat always get more out of their followers than those who offer safety and a good time. When it comes to the pinch, human beings are heroic.

—GEORGE ORWELL

Valor delights in the test.

—PROVERB

Sometimes even to live is an act of courage.

—SENECA

They are surely to be esteemed the bravest spirits who, having the clearest sense of both the pains and pleasures of life, do not on that account shrink from danger.

—THUCYDIDES

Be not afraid of greatness: some are born great, some achieve greatness, and some have greatness thrust upon them.

—WILLIAM SHAKESPEARE, *TWELFTH NIGHT*

We do not admire a man of timid peace.

—THEODORE ROOSEVELT

The courage we desire and prize is not the courage to die decently, but to live manfully.
—THOMAS CARLYLE

For without belittling the courage with which men have died, we should not forget those acts of courage with which men...have *lived*.
—JOHN F. KENNEDY

The paradox of courage is that a man must be a little careless of his life in order to keep it.
—G.K. CHESTERTON

Courage charms us, because it indicates that a man loves an idea better than all things in the world, that he is thinking neither of his bed, nor his dinner, nor his money, but will venture all to put in act the invisible thought of his mind.
—RALPH WALDO EMERSON

You gain strength, courage and confidence by every experience in which you really stop to look fear in the face. You must do the thing you think you cannot do.

—ELEANOR ROOSEVELT

Aggressive fighting for the right is the greatest sport in the world.

—THEODORE ROOSEVELT

Bravery never goes out of fashion.

—WILLIAM M. THACKERAY

Perfect courage is to do without witnesses what one would be capable of doing with the world looking on.

—FRANCOIS, DUC DE LA ROCHEFOUCAULD

There is plenty of courage among us for the abstract but not for the concrete.

—HELEN KELLER

Few are willing to brave the disapproval of their fellows, the censure of their colleagues, the wrath of their society. Moral courage is a rarer commodity than bravery in battle or great intelligence. Yet it is the one essential vital quality for those who seek to change a world that yields most painfully to change.

—ROBERT F. KENNEDY

Facing it—always facing it—that's the way to get through. Face it!

—JOSEPH CONRAD

COMPASSION

What do we live for if it is not to make life less difficult for each other?

—GEORGE ELIOT

No ceremony that to great ones 'longs,
Not the king's crown, nor the deputed sword,
The marshal's truncheon, nor the judge's robe,
Become them with the one half so good a grace
As mercy does.

—WILLIAM SHAKESPEARE, *MEASURE FOR MEASURE*

When I was young, I admired clever people. Now that I am old, I admire kind people.

—RABBI ABRAHAM JOSHUA HESCHEL

Without justice, courage is weak.

—BENJAMIN FRANKLIN

Kind words can be short and easy to speak, but their echoes are truly endless.

—MOTHER THERESA

I sought for the greatness and genius of America in her commodious harbors and her ample rivers—and it was not there...in her fertile fields and boundless forests—and it was not there...in her rich mines and her vast world commerce—and it was not there...in her democratic Congress and her matchless Constitution—and it was not there. Not until I went into the churches of America and heard her pulpits flame with righteousness did I understand the secret of her genius and power. America is great because she is good, and if America ever ceases to be good, America will cease to be great.

—ALEXIS DE TOCQUEVILLE

POSTERITY

Lives of great men all remind us
We can make our lives sublime,
And, departing, leave behind us
Footprints on the sands of time.
—HENRY WADSWORTH LONGFELLOW

No man is truly great who is great only in his life-time. The test of greatness is the page of history.
—WILLIAM HAZLITT

I do the very best I know how—the very best I can; and mean to keep doing so until the end. If the end brings me out all right, what is said against me won't amount to anything. If the end brings me out wrong, ten angels swearing I was right would make no difference.
—ABRAHAM LINCOLN

To go against the dominant thinking of your friends, of most of the people you see every day, is perhaps the most difficult act of heroism you can perform.

—THEODORE H. WHITE

Noble deeds are most estimable when hidden.

—BLAISE PASCAL

Difficulty is the excuse history never accepts.

—EDWARD R. MURROW

My rule, in which I have always found satisfaction, is, never to turn aside in public affairs through views of private interest; but to go straight forward in doing what appears to me right at the time, leaving the consequences with Providence.

—BENJAMIN FRANKLIN

I am certain that after the dust of centuries has passed over our cities, we, too, will be remembered not for victories or defeats in battle or politics, but for our contribution to the human spirit.
—JOHN F. KENNEDY

If any man seeks for greatness, let him forget greatness and ask for truth, and he will find both.
—HORACE MANN

Fame usually comes to those who are thinking about something else.
—OLIVER WENDELL HOLMES, SR.

The opportunist thinks of me and today. The statesman thinks of us and tomorrow.
—DWIGHT D. EISENHOWER

The final test of a leader is that he leaves behind in other men the conviction and the will to carry on.

—WALTER LIPPMANN

I sometimes think that great men are like great mountains: one cannot realize their greatness till one stands at some distance from them.

—JOSEPH CHAMBERLAIN

The difference between a politician and a statesman is: a politician thinks of the next election and a statesman thinks of the next generation.

—JAMES FREEMAN CLARKE

If you think too much about being re-elected, it is very difficult to be worth re-electing.

—WOODROW WILSON

SERVICE

And when we think we lead, we are most led.

—LORD BYRON

We, the people, elect leaders not to rule but to serve.

—DWIGHT D. EISENHOWER

The superior man is easy to serve and difficult to please.

—CONFUCIUS

The man who commands efficiently must have obeyed others in the past, and the man who obeys dutifully is worthy of being some day a commander.

—CICERO

I am convinced that the best service a retired general can perform is to turn in his tongue along with his suit, and to mothball his opinions.

—OMAR N. BRADLEY

In a democracy, a man who does not listen cannot lead.

—DAVID S. BRODER

We cannot all be masters, nor all masters
Cannot be truly followed.

—WILLIAM SHAKESPEARE, *OTHELLO*

My joy in learning is partly that it enables me to teach.

—SENECA

The administration of government, like a guardianship, ought to be directed to the good of those who confer, not of those who receive the trust.

—CICERO

The future lies with those wise political leaders who realize that the great public is interested more in government than in politics.

—FRANKLIN D. ROOSEVELT

Leadership is solving problems. The day soldiers stop bringing you their problems is the day you have stopped leading them. They have either lost confidence that you can help or concluded you do not care. Either case is a failure of leadership.

—COLIN POWELL

There is no cause half so sacred as the cause of a people. There is no idea so uplifting as the idea of the service of humanity.

—WOODROW WILSON

If we do not lay out ourselves in the service of mankind whom should we serve?

—ABIGAIL ADAMS

I expect to pass through life but once. If, therefore, there be any kindness I can show, or any good thing I can do for any fellow being, let me do it now...as I shall not pass this way again.

—WILLIAM PENN

Government includes the art of formulating a policy, and using the political technique to attain so much of that policy as will receive general support; persuading, leading, sacrificing, teaching always, because the greatest duty of any statesman is to educate.

—FRANKLIN D. ROOSEVELT

There are two ways of spreading light: to be the candle or the mirror that reflects it.

—EDITH WHARTON

The time is always right to do what is right.

—REV. MARTIN LUTHER KING, JR.

Finally, whether you are citizens of America or citizens of the world, ask of us the same high standards of strength and sacrifice which we ask of you. With a good conscience our only sure reward, with history the final judge of our deeds, let us go forth to lead the land we love, asking His blessing and His help, but knowing that here on earth God's work must truly be our own.

—JOHN F. KENNEDY

When you teach your son, you teach your son's son.

—THE TALMUD

True heroism is remarkably sober, very undramatic. It is not the urge to surpass all others at whatever cost, but the urge to serve others at whatever cost.

—ARTHUR ASHE

VISION

If a man hasn't discovered something that he will die for, he isn't fit to live.

—REV. MARTIN LUTHER KING, JR.

Where there is no vision, the people perish.

—PROVERBS 29:18

Political ability is the ability to foretell what is going to happen tomorrow, next week, next month and next year. And to have the ability afterwards to explain why it didn't happen.

—WINSTON CHURCHILL

Those who spend their time on small things usually become incapable of large ones.

—FRANCOIS, DUC DE LA ROCHEFOUCAULD

Just because a man lacks the use of his eyes doesn't mean he lacks vision.

—STEVIE WONDER

Nothing happens unless first a dream.

—CARL SANDBURG

How far would Moses have gone if he had taken a poll in Egypt?

—HARRY S. TRUMAN

Great things are not something accidental, but must certainly be willed.

—VINCENT VAN GOGH

The right man comes at the right time.

—ITALIAN PROVERB

A genuine leader is not a searcher for consensus
but a molder of consensus.

—REV. MARTIN LUTHER KING, JR.

WISDOM

The test of a first-rate intelligence is the ability to hold two opposed ideas in the mind at the same time, and still retain the ability to function.

—F. SCOTT FITZGERALD

The true statesman does not despise any wisdom, howsoever lowly may be its origin.

—MARK TWAIN

Magnanimity in politics is not seldom the truest wisdom; and a great empire and little minds go ill together.

—EDMUND BURKE

In the place where there is a leader, do not seek to become a leader. In the place where there is no leader, strive to become a leader.

—THE TALMUD

Great men undertake great things because they are great; and fools because they think them easy.

—MARQUIS DE VAUVENARGUES

To-day a reader, to-morrow a leader.

—W. FUSSELMAN

It is high time that we had lights that are not incendiary torches.

—GEORGE SAND

One cool judgment is worth a thousand hasty counsels. The thing to be supplied is light, not heat.

—WOODROW WILSON

If you command wisely, you'll be obeyed cheerfully.

—THOMAS FULLER

Let the people know the truth and the country is safe.

—ABRAHAM LINCOLN

I have one request: may I never use my reason against truth.

—ELIE WIESEL

Good education is the essential foundation of a strong democracy.

—BARBARA BUSH

Of all paths a man could strike into, there is, at any given moment, a best path, which, here and now, it were of all things wisest for him to do. To find this path, and walk in it, is the one thing needful for him.

—THOMAS CARLYLE

→ POWER

What you cannot enforce, do not command.
—SOPHOCLES

The renown of great men should always be measured by the means which they have used to acquire it.
—FRANCOIS, DUC DE LA ROCHEFOUCAULD

[The tyrant] is always stirring up some war or another, in order that the people may require a leader.
—PLATO

Every country is renewed out of the unknown ranks and not out of the ranks of those already famous and powerful and in control.
—WOODROW WILSON

There are some whom the applause of the multitude has deluded into the belief that they are really statesmen.

—PLATO

Do not hold the delusion that your advancement is accomplished by crushing others.

—CICERO

In times of peace the people look most to their representatives; but in war, to the executive solely.

—THOMAS JEFFERSON

Uneasy lies the head that wears a crown.
—WILLIAM SHAKESPEARE, *HENRY VI, Part II*

A man who enjoys responsibility usually gets it. A man who merely likes exercising authority usually loses it.

—MALCOLM S. FORBES

Power...is not an end in itself, but is an instrument that must be used toward an end.

—JEANE J. KIRKPATRICK

Asking "Who ought to be boss?" is like asking "Who ought to be the tenor in the quartet?" Obviously, the man who can sing tenor.

—HENRY FORD

To be a king and wear a crown is more glorious to them that see it than it is pleasure to them that bear it.

—ELIZABETH I

There is something behind the throne greater than the king himself.

—WILLIAM PITT

Elected leaders who forget how they got there won't the next time.

—MALCOLM S. FORBES

A leader who does not hesitate before he sends his nation into battle is not fit to be a leader.

—GOLDA MEIR

Power tends to corrupt, and absolute power corrupts absolutely.

—LORD ACTON

There is no happiness for people at the expense of other people.

—ANWAR EL-SADAT

The subject's love is the king's best guard.

—THOMAS FULLER

Ill can he rule the great that cannot reach the small.

—EDMUND SPENCER

You can build a throne with bayonets, but you can't sit on it for long.

—BORIS YELTSIN

CONVICTION

Never, "for the sake of peace and quiet," deny your own experience and convictions.
—DAG HAMMARSKJOLD

What is the essence of kingship? [It is] to rule oneself well, and not be led astray by wealth or fame.
—APOCRYPHA, LETTER OF ARISTEAS, NO. 178

Important principles may and must be inflexible.
—ABRAHAM LINCOLN

The secret of success is constancy to purpose.
—BENJAMIN DISRAELI

If we are to be a really great people, we must strive in good faith to play a great part in the world. We cannot avoid meeting great issues. All that we can determine for ourselves is whether we shall meet them well or ill.

—THEODORE ROOSEVELT

As I would not be a slave, so I would not be a master. This expresses my idea of democracy.

—ABRAHAM LINCOLN

Democracy is based upon the conviction that there are extraordinary possibilities in ordinary people.

—HARRY EMERSON FOSDICK

We must not in the course of public life expect immediate approbation and immediate grateful acknowledgment of our services. But let us persevere through abuse and even injury. The internal satisfaction of a good conscience is always present, and time will do us justice in the minds of the people, even those at present the most prejudiced against us.

—BENJAMIN FRANKLIN

If I also, perhaps, stood before the prospect of finding myself in a minority of *one* voice, I humbly believe that I would have the courage to remain in such a hopeless minority. This is for me the only truthful position.

—MAHATMA GANDHI

Every generation of Americans needs to know that freedom consists not in doing what we like, but in having the right to do what we ought.

—POPE JOHN PAUL II

Essential characteristics of a gentleman: The will to put himself in the place of others; the horror of forcing others into positions from which he would himself recoil; the power to do what seems to him to be right, without considering what others may say or think.

—JOHN GALSWORTHY

The true idealist pursues what his heart says is right in a way that his head says will work.

—RICHARD M. NIXON

When people are least sure, they are often most dogmatic.

—JOHN KENNETH GALBRAITH

The thing always happens that you really believe in; and the belief in a thing makes it happen.

—FRANK LLOYD WRIGHT

Faith in oneself…is the best and safest course.

—MICHELANGELO

Don't foul, don't flinch—hit the line hard.

—THEODORE ROOSEVELT

The worth of every conviction consists precisely in the steadfastness with which it is held.
—JANE ADAMS

It is easy in the world to live after the world's opinion; it is easy in solitude to live after our own; but the great man is he who in the midst of the crowd keeps with perfect sweetness the independence of solitude.
—RALPH WALDO EMERSON

Those who believe that they are exclusively in the right are generally those who achieve something.
—ALDOUS HUXLEY

Let me tell you the secret that has led me to my goal: my strength lies solely in my tenacity.
—LOUIS PASTEUR

$\longrightarrow$ **ACTION**

The test of any man lies in action.

—PINDAR

Let him that would move the world, first move himself.

—SOCRATES

He who hesitates is last.

—MAE WEST

Not the cry, but the flight of the wild duck, leads the flock to fly and follow.

—CHINESE PROVERB

Every new day begins with possibilities. It's up to us to fill it with the things that move us toward progress and peace.

—RONALD REAGAN

The great end of life is not knowledge but action.

—T.H. HUXLEY

Think like a man of action, act like a man of thought.

—HENRI BERGSON

Every great action is extreme when it is undertaken. Only after it has been accomplished does it seem possible to those creatures of more common stuff.

—STENDHAL

If you can't feed a hundred people, then feed just one.

—MOTHER THERESA

Example moves the world more than doctrine.

—HENRY MILLER

You can preach a better sermon with your life than with your lips.

—OLIVER GOLDSMITH

It is nothing to give pension and cottage to the widow who has lost her son; it is nothing to give food and medicine to the workman who has broken his arm, or the decrepit woman wasting in sickness. But it is something to use your time and strength to war with the waywardness and thoughtlessness of mankind; to keep the erring workman in your service till you have made him an unerring one, and to direct your fellow-merchant to the opportunity which his judgment would have lost.

—JOHN RUSKIN

Don't hit at all if it is honorably possible to avoid hitting; but never hit soft.

—THEODORE ROOSEVELT

So what do we do? Anything. Something. So long as we just don't sit there. If we screw it up, start over. Try something else. If we wait until we've satisfied all the uncertainties, it may be too late.

—LEE IACOCCA

One can never consent to creep when one feels an impulse to soar.

—HELEN KELLER

You can't build a reputation on what you are going to do.

—HENRY FORD

⟶ **WORK**

I do not know anyone who has got to the top without hard work. That is the recipe. It will not always get you to the top, but should get you pretty near.

—MARGARET THATCHER

The higher men climb the longer their working day...There are no office hours for leaders.

—CARDINAL GIBBONS

No great thing is created suddenly.

—EPICTETUS

When work goes out of style, we may expect to see civilization totter and fall.

—JOHN D. ROCKEFELLER

Kings are like stars—they rise and set, they have
The worship of the world, but no repose.

—PERCY BYSSHE SHELLEY

But the virtues we acquire by first exercising them, as is the case with all the arts, for it is by doing what we ought to do when we have learnt the arts that we learn the arts themselves; we become builders by building and harpists by playing the harp. Similarly it is by doing just acts that we become just, by doing temperate acts that we become temperate, by doing courageous acts that we become courageous.

—ARISTOTLE

It is the duty of government to make it difficult for people to do wrong, easy to do right.

—WILLIAM E. GLADSTONE

Big shots are little shots who kept shooting.

—CHRISTOPHER MORLEY

The reward for work well done is the opportunity to do more.

—JONAS SALK, M.D.

Work is something you can count on, a trusted, lifelong friend who never deserts you.

—MARGARET BOURKE-WHITE

The work will teach you how to do it.

—ESTONIAN PROVERB

If you could make a pudding wi' thinking o' the batter, it 'ud be easy getting dinner.

—GEORGE ELIOT

Miracles sometimes occur, but one has to work terribly hard for them.

—CHAIM WEIZMANN

You don't just luck into things...You build step by step, whether it's friendships or opportunities.
—BARBARA BUSH

Laziness may appear attractive, but work gives satisfaction.
—ANNE FRANK

Perseverance is the hard work you do after you get tired of doing the hard work you already did.
—NEWT GINGRICH

If opportunity doesn't knock, build a door.
—MILTON BERLE

INSPIRATION

No man is great enough or wise enough for any of us to surrender our destiny to. The only way in which anyone can lead us is to restore to us the belief in our own guidance.

—HENRY MILLER

There are some men who lift the age they inhabit, till all men walk on higher ground in that lifetime.

—MAXWELL ANDERSON

But screw your courage to the sticking-place, And we'll not fail.

—WILLIAM SHAKESPEARE, *MACBETH*

A leader is a dealer in hope.

—NAPOLEON BONAPARTE

A man is not as big as his belief in himself; he is as big as the number of persons who believe in him.

—WOODROW WILSON

I've always felt that a manager has achieved a great deal when he's able to motivate one other person. When it comes to making the place run, motivation is everything. You might be able to do the work of two people, but you can't be two people. Instead, you have to inspire the next guy down the line and get him to inspire his people.

—LEE IACOCCA

It was the nation and the race dwelling all round the globe that had the lion's heart. I had the luck to be called upon to give the roar.

—WINSTON CHURCHILL

Leadership appears to be the art of getting others to want to do something you are convinced should be done.

—VANCE PACKARD

Not he is great who can alter matter, but he who can alter my state of mind.

—RALPH WALDO EMERSON

With public sentiment, nothing can fail; without it, nothing can succeed. Consequently he who molds public sentiment goes deeper than he who enacts statutes or pronounces decisions.

—ABRAHAM LINCOLN

You know what makes leadership? It is the ability to get men to do what they don't want to do, and like it.

—HARRY S. TRUMAN

When you reach for the stars, you may not quite get one, but you won't come up with a handful of mud either.

—LEO BURNETT

No leader can be too far ahead of his followers.

—ELEANOR ROOSEVELT

Great men are the guide-posts and landmarks in the state.

—EDMUND BURKE

A pat on the back, though only a few vertebrae removed from a kick in the pants, is miles ahead in results.

—BENNETT CERF

Keep your eyes on the stars, and your feet on the ground.

—THEODORE ROOSEVELT

A great manager has a knack for making ball-players think they are better than they think they are. He forces you to have a good opinion of yourself. He lets you know he believes in you. He makes you get more out of yourself. And once you learn how good you really are, you never settle for playing anything less than your very best.

—REGGIE JACKSON

Hold fast to dreams, for if dreams die,
Life is a broken-winged bird that cannot fly.

—LANGSTON HUGHES

Keep away from people who try to belittle your ambitions. Small people always do that, but the really great make you feel that you, too, can become great.

—MARK TWAIN

Example is not the main thing in influencing others. It is the only thing.

—ALBERT SCHWEITZER

Each man is a hero and an oracle to somebody.

—RALPH WALDO EMERSON

Every individual has a place to fill in the world, and is important in some respect, whether he chooses to be so or not.

—NATHANIEL HAWTHORNE

CHANGE

A great statesman is he who knows when to depart from traditions, as well as when to adhere to them.

—JOHN STUART MILL

A disposition to preserve, and an ability to improve, taken together, would be my standard of a statesman.

—EDMUND BURKE

Only in growth, reform, and change, paradoxically enough, is true security to be found.

—ANNE MORROW LINDBERGH

We must become the change we want to see.

—MAHATMA GANDHI

A foolish consistency is the hobgoblin of little minds, adored by little statesmen and philosophers and divines. With consistency a great soul has simply nothing to do. He may as well concern himself with his shadow on the wall. Speak what you think now in hard words and tomorrow speak what tomorrow thinks in hard words again, though it contradict everything you said today...Is it so bad then to be misunderstood? Pythagoras was misunderstood, and Socrates, and Jesus, and Luther, and Copernicus, and Galileo, and Newton, and every pure and wise spirit that ever took flesh.
To be great is to be misunderstood.

—RALPH WALDO EMERSON

Only with a new ruler do you realize the value of the old.

—BURMESE PROVERB

Whenever an individual or a business decides that success has been attained, progress stops.

—THOMAS J. WATSON

Like all weak men he laid an exaggerated stress on not changing one's mind.

—SOMERSET MAUGHAM

Consistency is the last refuge of the unimaginative.

—OSCAR WILDE

The world is round and the place which may seem like the end, may also be only the beginning.

—IVY BAKER PRIEST

There is no miraculous change that takes place in a boy that makes him a man. He becomes a man by being a man.

—LOUIS L'AMOUR

If you want to make enemies, try to change something.

—WOODROW WILSON

Non-violence is the first article of my faith. It is also the last article of my creed.

—MAHATMA GANDHI

THE OVAL OFFICE

No man will ever bring out of the Presidency
the reputation which carries him into it.

—THOMAS JEFFERSON

The presidency is more than an honor. It is more
than an office. It is a charge to keep, and I will
give it my all.

—GEORGE W. BUSH

Oh, that lovely title, ex-President.

—DWIGHT D. EISENHOWER

I have been told I was on the road to hell, but
I had no idea it was just a mile down the road
with a Dome on it.

—ABRAHAM LINCOLN

Sleep not when others speak, sit not when others stand, speak not when you should hold your peace, walk not when others stop.
—GEORGE WASHINGTON

I think this is the most extraordinary collection of talent, of human knowledge, that has ever been gathered together at the White House, with the possible exception of when Thomas Jefferson dined alone.
—JOHN F. KENNEDY

There is a natural aristocracy among men. The grounds of this are virtue and talent.
—THOMAS JEFFERSON

RISK

Take calculated risks. That is quite different from being rash.

—GEN. GEORGE S. PATTON

Never let the fear of striking out get in your way.

—BABE RUTH

We may make mistakes—but they must never be mistakes which result from faintness of heart or abandonment of moral principle.

—FRANKLIN D. ROOSEVELT

Far better it is to dare mighty things, to win glorious triumphs, even though checkered by failure, than to take rank with those poor spirits who neither enjoy much nor suffer much, because they live in the gray twilight that knows not victory nor defeat.

—THEODORE ROOSEVELT

Only those who dare to fail greatly can ever achieve greatly.

—ROBERT F. KENNEDY

All of the great leaders have had one characteristic in common: it was the willingness to confront unequivocally the major anxiety of their people in their time. This, and not much else, is the essence of leadership.

—JOHN KENNETH GALBRAITH

The most prominent place in hell is reserved for those who are neutral on the great issues of life.

—REV. BILLY GRAHAM

Hell, there are no rules here—we're trying to accomplish something.

—THOMAS ALVA EDISON

Don't be afraid to take a big step if one is indicated. You can't cross a chasm in two small jumps.

—DAVID LLOYD GEORGE

FAILURE

I don't know the key to success, but the key to failure is trying to please everybody.

—BILL COSBY

Imagine a congress of eminent celebrities such as More, Bacon, Grotius, Pascal, Cromwell, Bossuet, Montesquieu, Jefferson, Napoleon, Pitt, etc. They would be an Encyclopedia of Errors.

—LORD ACTON

Flops are a part of life's menu, and I've never been a girl to miss out on any of the courses.

—ROSALIND RUSSELL

A chief is a man who assumes responsibility. He says, "I was beaten." He does not say, "My men were beaten." Thus speaks a real man.

—ANTOINE DE SAINT-EXUPÉRY

TEAMWORK

When the best leader's work is done, the people say, "We did it ourselves."

—LAO-TZU

We can't all be heroes because somebody has to sit on the curb and clap as they go by.

—WILL ROGERS

There is a point, of course, where a man must take the isolated peak and break with all his associates for clear principle; but until that time comes he must work, if he would be of use, with men as they are. As long as the good in them overbalances the evil, let him work with them for the best that can be obtained.

—THEODORE ROOSEVELT

When we lost I couldn't sleep at night. When we win, I can't sleep at night. But when you win, you wake up feeling better.

—JOE TORRE

A small group of thoughtful people could change the world. Indeed, it's the only thing that ever has.

—MARGARET MEAD

I long to accomplish a great and noble task, but it is my chief duty to accomplish humble tasks as though they were great and noble. The world is moved along not only by the mighty shoves of its heroes but also by the aggregate of the tiny pushes of each honest worker.

—HELEN KELLER

Never tell people how to do things. Tell them what to do and they will surprise you with their ingenuity.

—GEN. GEORGE S. PATTON

A leader should not get too far in front of his troops or he will be shot in the ass.

—JOSEPH CLARK

The best executive is the one who has sense enough to pick good men to do what he wants done, and self-restraint enough to keep from meddling with them while they do it.

—THEODORE ROOSEVELT

First-rate men hire first-rate men; second-rate men hire third-rate men.

—LEO ROSTEN

Great men are rarely isolated mountain-peaks; they are the summits of ranges.

—THOMAS WENTWORTH HIGGINSON

If I have seen further, it is by standing on the shoulders of giants.

—ISAAC NEWTON

It is amazing what you can accomplish if you do not care who gets the credit.

—HARRY S. TRUMAN

Democracy is the worst system devised by the wit of man, except for all the others.

—WINSTON CHURCHILL

How can you govern a nation that has two hundred and forty-six different kinds of cheese?

—CHARLES DE GAULLE

To disagree, one doesn't have to be disagreeable.

—BARRY M. GOLDWATER

CHALLENGE

There aren't any great men. There are just great challenges that ordinary men like you and me are forced by circumstances to meet.

—ADM. WILLIAM F. HALSEY

He is the best sailor who can steer within fewest points of the wind, and exact a motive power out of the greatest obstacles.

—HENRY DAVID THOREAU

I tell you that as long as I can conceive something better than myself I cannot be easy unless I am striving to bring it into existence or clearing the way for it.

—GEORGE BERNARD SHAW

Great spirits have always found violent opposition from mediocrities.

—ALBERT EINSTEIN

The man who is swimming against the stream knows the strength of it.

—WOODROW WILSON

High expectations are the key to everything.

—SAM WALTON

If you think you can win, you can win. Faith is necessary to victory.

—WILLIAM HAZLITT

It is at night that faith in light is admirable.

—EDMOND ROSTAND

SELF-KNOWLEDGE

Greatness knows itself.
—WILLIAM SHAKESPEARE, *HENRY IV, Part I*

We succeed in enterprises which demand the positive qualities we possess, but we excel in those which can also make use of our defects.
—ALEXIS DE TOCQUEVILLE

When a man realizes his littleness, his greatness can appear.
—H.G. WELLS

He who reigns within himself, and rules passions, desires, and fears, is more than a king.
—JOHN MILTON

Knowing what you can *not* do is more important than knowing what you can do. In fact, that's good taste.

—LUCILLE BALL

He who comes up to his own idea of greatness must always have had a very low standard of it in his head.

—WILLIAM HAZLITT

Great men never feel great; small men never feel small.

—CHINESE PROVERB

He that would govern others, first should be Master of himself.

—PHILIP MASSINGER

Men can starve from a lack of self-realization as much as they can from a lack of bread.

—RICHARD WRIGHT

Millions of individuals making their own decisions in the marketplace will always allocate resources better than any centralized government planning process.

—RONALD REAGAN

I don't like myself, I'm crazy about myself.

—MAE WEST

Know thyself.

—SOCRATES